AFTER EARTH

After Earth

POEMS

Michael Lavers

UNIVERSITY OF TAMPA PRESS

Manufactured in the United States of America
Printed on acid-free paper ∞
First Edition

On the Cover:
Igor Nekraha, "Clear Evening," acrylic on canvas, 23.6 x 23.6 inches.
Copyright © 2019 by Igor Nekraha. All rights reserved.
Reproduced by permission of the artist.

Cover design by Joshua Steward and Richard Mathews

The University of Tampa Press
401 West Kennedy Boulevard
Tampa, FL 33606

ISBN 978-159732-172-3(pbk.)
ISBN 978-159732-171-6 (hbk.)

Library of Congress Control Number: 2018932504

Browse & order online at
http://utpress.ut.edu

Library of Congress Cataloging-in-Publication Data

Names: Lavers, Michael, 1983- author.
Title: After earth : poems / Michael Lavers.
Description: First edition. | Tampa, FL : University of Tampa Press, [2019]
    |Identifiers: LCCN 2019040209 (print) | LCCN 2019040210 (ebook) | ISBN
    9781597321716 (hardback ; acid-free paper) | ISBN 9781597321723 (trade
    paperback ; acid-free paper) | ISBN 9781597321730 (ebook)
Subjects: LCGFT: Poetry.
Classification: LCC PS3612.A944243 A68 2019 (print) | LCC PS3612.A944243
    (ebook) | DDC 811/.6--dc23
LC record available at https://lccn.loc.gov/2019040209
LC ebook record available at https://lccn.loc.gov/2019040210

Contents

·ı|||ıı·

For Claire.
And for Isaak and Magda.

AFTER EARTH

Instead of a Lullaby

I wanted more than a world for you,
more than a life.

But here we are. Outside
your window is a garden, and a table,

and the wedges of the orange
that you left there, fuming in the cold.

There's time,
and so there is a need
to be precise, to count our seconds
or our years together,

fuming pieces of this accidental world,
and cast off from a vast compactness,

that which led you here, exhausted,
unforeshadowed, radiant, and strange

as water flowing over sheets of gold.

Already you know seven constellations
and two types of cloud,

the path between the honeysuckle and the pines,

the poison ivy, and those yellow moths,
and how there's nothing new

but in the old sense that the moon is new
and yet a ruin.

You know the concrete room
of consciousness through which seeps

January light, the sound of snow under your feet,
the moan and hum of Homer,
                          and a ricochet of phrases

from "The House Was Quiet and the World Was Calm."

You know this moment, which I thought
had warmth in it, and light, and space—

enough to sing you something in—
                              is simply smoke,
and gone before I even started speaking.

All the cowslips and clematis we ran through
are gone; so are the night trills of the nuthatch,

and the smell of ferns. The swaths of geese,
the cherry blossoms, and those spotted frogs.

If I could mend what has been shattered,

or if I could gently, gently reassemble air,
if I remembered clearly, and could tell you everything,

then we could listen to the nighthawks dart and hum,
then part in peace.
                    We carry nothing
from the fire of years except the smoke of things,

this crude transcription of a breathing-space,
a sketch of bread and fire and rain,
some sounds to decorate our distances:

"The moon is white," "The clouds move with the wind."

"It is a beauteous evening, calm and free . . ."

If I could breathe
more than a breath, and stir the empty opus

up ahead of us, praising those silences
outside the vain and sticky tedium of living;

if I could say, ok,
                        let there be light
even without your pupil and its crystal vase—.

But mostly I try keeping quiet,
                        and then fail.

I'm bad at turning what is wavering
or tattered into permanence, and cannot sing to you

as if these words might lend you breath
since they take it away.

                        But that we coincide,
here, for the moment, must be written down,
before the end.

That much, I promise, isn't decorative.

We speak and speak; the stars don't flinch.
The universe exhales; we tremble, and are changed.

What we accumulate is dust, but it has shape
and mass and a duration under heaven.

Angels and ministers of grace defend us—

who's to say? But sometimes

in the night's thick velvet, openings appear:
this snow, that bowl of oranges, those stars.

Your Father at Fourteen

Already tall, all femur and no thigh,
and tripping on my shadow like a new giraffe.
Not your father, but his epigraph,

and not the rider, but the rider's horse, just feeding
my way through the universe. My eyes
a dirty gas-stove blue, my hair as thick and dirty

as those Van Gogh brushstrokes flecked with soil,
shipwrecked bugs, whatever wafted
through that blue French air. I'd walk

to where the wind huddled for warmth
inside the harbour, carrying some comic in my coat,
and smash glass bottles on the pier till I got caught,

perfecting my ambition and regret,
miming rebellion with a fescue cigarette.
I knew the names of birds, but not their calls,

not girls, only their garish names,
which I could coax, if I repeated them,
to drop their living referents like a dress,

revealing stranger nakedness,
and rhythms as translucent as a fire ant's wing.
I couldn't see the ocean from my window,

but could smell its salt, and sometimes hear
the surf revving its engine, stalling eddies
and loquacious jets, the Narrows where

I once hauled up an oxblood octopus,
slashed badly by the hook, and saw
my own reflection settle like a bruise

into its coiling polaroid of skin.
This was the one past I was in.
I spat, and sluffed, and copiously slept,

I slept as if a mustache could be spun from sleep,
or sleep might sugar and ferment even the air
to muscle. I multiplied my best joy

by my hardest grief, and chose to like it here:
the long, dark, winter afternoons, the way
the mayflies hatched in vetch; I wasn't mortal yet:

I hadn't watched you first chew honeydew
or warmed this cup of milk to coax you back to bed.
But one day late in March, I thought, almost, of you:

the adults placed their bets on when the ice
over the lake would break and take the junk cars
left to sink. I dared myself to walk out there,

and got halfway before a long, low groan
revealed a universe of cracks and coming aftershocks.
The ice hummed like a song that I could feel

would end, and soon, bringing the future
with it, shapeless as the teal-grey water,
shadowy, and bright, and almost real.

On Water, in Childhood

How it would fall
and fill, and freeze and flow, or shimmer
or surround or slake; and how it heaved,
collapsed, cascaded, how it blazed, carving
the cold and high-dunned beaches of my boyhood,
how it breathed, becoming less than air,
and breathed again and fell again, transparent
as a mirror, moving, still, the way
it slid and stirred beneath my uncle's boat,
alive and writhing as it buoyed us,
diffusing fringe greens into rusty blues,
the whitecaps breaking on the sandstone bluffs,
the sudden fords, peninsulas, and shallows,
Margarets Bay, the delta's ventricles
and the chambered cave. And how one day I slipped
from stern and fell into a tar-black world
of it, unnoticed, taken in like water pouring
into water, panic fading fast
to feeling I had tarried long already
and could now clear space for its cold lull,
a rhythm whose faint edge touched everything,
its wake and welter and its noiseless pull,
and how that pull wasn't pumped out of me
that day but stayed, and rises when I wade
into it, when I put it in my mouth,
whenever I am sick of shivering
or shore and wish for nothing more than to be
hushed and steadied, healed, held, dissolved.

Andromache's Lullaby

Son, no helmet or horse
can rearrange the stars
once Venus shifts her course
to better flirt with Mars.

When wind that storms the tower
pauses, you might hear
some godly homesick warrior
sharpening a spear,

and squeals as buzzards feed.
Even the sun goes down.
Even hawks retreat.
So take off your tired toy crown

and sleep, and if you grow
up tall enough to wield
your father's sword, I'll sew
silk armbands for a shield.

If not, the gods know best,
and taper your lamp's flame;
there are worse beds than dust,
and better fates than fame.

For what good is a hero,
what evil can spears destroy,
when every ground is zero,
and every heart a Troy?

Cosmography

In one, a cesspool stirred to lamentation.
In one, a vacant palace and a throne
deposed by air that would step down
if it could be mere breath again. In one,
all hours coalesce, like insects hatching
on a standing pond, while in another,
they make a single-file break for it
over the barbed-wired hills. No stars in one,
or else no moon, or else no sun, or else
two suns, stabbing their spurs into the earth.
Some just like ours, except for wind, and rain,
and some where starlight drips like resin
from cracked wood, and gravity relaxes
its long tenure on the leaves, and someone
makes a greenish fire for us from the firs.
The one where silver moths will cover you
like cloth until your shivering has stopped,
then fly, blushing, away. The ones where
I can find you, and the ones where I run
through the dunes, calling your name, hearing
the darkness take it, and the boiling sea.
One with a fountain. One with a cloud.

Abridged Taxonomy of Light

Some light unfurls enormous wings,
as though sunning itself. Some light
just roosts, grooming its blue and thinning

plumage down to stars. Some evenings,
even waning sun will overrun the atmosphere's
cracked dish, or else the dark will whisper

to the skull like waves slowly devouring a cliff.
Sometimes September shifts its weight
onto unwinnowed wheat and spins out gold,

gamboge, champagne, chartreuse.
Sometimes the Earth and this whole edge
of space seem like the blast of chaff

after whatever midnight mass of nothingness
or suns there was before this mess began,
that hornets' nest of silhouette and shade.

But somewhere light grows cold, and heavy,
and condenses to a river whose vast delta
feeds whole galaxies of coral seas,

thicker forests, greener trees, and eyes
more clear and cavernous than these.

The Angel in Charge of Creating Earth Addresses His Cohort

Who cares if more important worlds have been
assigned to those more skillful, who make crusts
that never crack, or plates too fixed to creep
or jostle or explode? Ours are the splendors
of the makeshift, of the good enough,
of cold May wind, wailing and barbed and riven,
coastlines ragged as a vulture's wing,
of maggots and voles, a vast legion of catalysts
and scavengers the top worlds are deprived of,
worlds where the joins are tight, with skies
unyieldingly cloudless, only blue.
Believe your errors, what they lead you to.
Those patches we forgot to water?
Call them deserts, hide there all our
misbegotten dregs, the scorpions
and saltbush beds, blind rats, weird toads.
What's perfect is by definition free
of difference—but uncountable and great
are the variations of failure. Take this ostrich,
my self-portrait: botched and brainless,
but still capturing my flouncy abandon,
my leathery grace. Take humans, no two cracked
the same, some warped or knotted, bent of back,
some dragging weak-seamed hearts toward stagnation.
Even the lava spreads its glaze in ways
that no trained hand could replicate,
a slow terrible fluency that bleeds and burps
and teaches those who live nearby to love

what ends, to build what walls they must,
to graft their growing hopes to gravity,
and move more upright through the tilted world.
Don't envy them, those better makers; let them
envy you, not doomed to mastery,
still stunned by your mistakes, the broken
pomp of cow, the fraying homespun jellyfish,
the accidents of beauty, which, once realized,
can never be forgotten or undone.

The Invention of Birds

*The last wire proved a delightful elevator to the bird's tail and at last
there stood before me the real manikin of a kingfisher!*
—John James Audubon

Let light come down from air and be made
still. Let it pose. Let speed rest now forever
as water and paint, and let there be

a book from which not one crest or frill
will ever go missing. Let there be pages which,
once finished, could save, may yet save,

something of the shadows on the wheat
which will, silently, go; marshes of song,
now muted, but now visible and fixed.

Let them fall gladly, never to fall again.
Let those still living seem like forgeries,
phantasmal, brief, first drafts compared to

these my colors never kissed by smoke or pellet,
quickness cornered and made mine, some
permanence that corresponds to no thing known.

Daedalus to Icarus, if He Had Survived

Forgive me.

I knew blood was heavy.

And that you would glimpse something more.

More than grass, more than stone.

A new realm just past the horizon.

But if it's there, we can't reach it.

So rest.

And when you are done resting, stand up.

That is even more daring.

Wings were light.

Now the burden of life must be shouldered.

Your back must be straight.

The stars look so close, but are not.

This is Earth. We must walk.

Alberta Psalm

Whoso offereth praise glorifieth me

I get it, Lord. Who doesn't want to be loved?
But you could pull my hide tight, string it up,
let cold wind strum me like barbed-wire,
or force the luciferine flatulence of toads
in heat to echo flattery, and still you'd feel
no bigger, big as you are, than the dungflies
and the yellowjackets saying grace
above the babysbreath and brome. Of praise,
there's never enough. I love the varicose,
tar-sanded creeks, October's vast ice-over,
all the graupel, snowsqualls, deep hoar, drift.
I love the slight chinook that's blown all week,
shooing the dirty clouds away, and fooling
bears to thinking spring is here, the rye
to spume and shed its crown of fumes.
But what else am I supposed to say? Well done?
Kudos to you? What do you need with all
that flattery? What is a trout's hymn
to a hawk? Or can the hare under the paw
be trusted if it says how sleek the lynx is?
Just how savvy can you be to make me
thrilled by so much less than you? These mushrooms,
for example, who have no need for heaven
to increase them if a hungry snail
or a warm, spore-spewing breeze will do.

The Peaceable Kingdom

It's back there, where we left it, cows still
strolling past the shops, red leaves still landing
on the garden paths, and Paradise Square
the way we knew it: passing but not past,
and not a place as much as an attempt
to hoard the rusting luster of the world.

Someone right now is changing reels
in the Princess Theatre, while someone else
peruses the bookstore where the soft chair
by the window is always empty, and a parrot
at the counter greets you quoting Dante
in Italian, English, Mandarin, and Cree.

And where are we? We left after our mother's
funeral, or our child's, and never returned.
Or we were exiled by our envy of the ranchers,
or of farther stars, or wandered through
the labyrinth of our agony or spite
until the silver thread of breath we trailed

snapped, stranding us here, at this bus station,
in the charred grass of Des Moines.
Des Moines is ok. The roads are potholed
and the schools are old, but still, we know
what's possible. Our hope, sometimes, is justified;
our grief, though constant, can be endured.

We know what we are missing—Judge Boon's
wisdom, Miss. Lane's generosity, Old Herman's
willingness to change his mind and keep
his dogs out back—but can't quite manage it,

although we have to try: more exiles join us
from that country every day. We keep the roads

plowed for them, when we can, rebuild
the schools, bind tomatoes, and make sure
the Blue Swan Bar is something they might
recognize: somebody sitting at the piano,
welcoming them in, striking that first
B minor chord of "Cracking Fire, Falling Snow."

Field Work

"Its form is that of a pastoral, easy, vulgar, and therefore disgusting..."

– Dr. Johnson

Description, description, adjective, noun:
this is a breeze. Look at Wetaskiwin,
this town I'm pumping gas in on my way
to somewhere real: a gaunt, dank-furred coyote
dozing on a greying plain, the runt spine
of its Main Street pocked with auto shops,
its houses painted anything from grey
to greyish beige, dead pickups sunk in bluegrass
like stray mammoths stuck in tar. Even
the light seems petrified and drifts like sand.
One hardware warehouse, one mink farm
gagging the clouds, one curling rink, one park,
its kept swan floating like a plastic bag.
What could be simpler?: step outside, say what
you see. A good life, since it has to be.
Maybe some token reference to Arcadia—
right here, or on its way; it doesn't matter:
paychecks come, or don't; trucks at the dump
move piles back and forth, keeping their ruin
straight. Even the teenagers, I see,
are happy here, in the available world—
the cars they rev at both the traffic lights
are relics hauled out of a golden age
into today: rusted and belching smoke,
but lavish in their way, blurry with bass,
Savini diamond rims spinning in place.

Coda

From the garden rose the sound of bees
that lurched and wobbled through the peonies.
We ate eggs and toast with milk that warmed
in minutes in the sun while fat drones swarmed
and looped like bullets misfired from the fields.
It was the sound the mind makes when it yields
to glutted blood. I didn't understand,
until one smelled the syrup on your hand,
and in a gold-encrusted drunken strut,
smeared pollen from its mandibles and gut
along your wrist. That morning you had tied
your hair, and as you rose and ran inside,
it gently bounced, and loosed, and then unfurled.
If the next is better, I'll still miss this world.

The Burden of Humans

The grass just has to wave, the birds just have
to sing. The grapes don't wonder what light is;
the light just lights them, and the grapes grape back.
The golden oaks just shed their summer dresses
on the lawn—but you? You have to read
Spinoza in the garden while the light
is good. You have to keep your focus as
the motorcycles scream out of the purple hills.
You have to sweat, and laugh, and weatherproof
the bedroom windows, and remember
names and dates, the town your parents met—
Milk River or Swan Hills?—and when they died,
you have to sweep the kitchen floor and then
define the good, the true, the beautiful,
or try, because azaleas can't see themselves,
the squirrels are busy, and the ferns have closed.
The frost tattoos its sermon on the rose,
but in a language only you can read;
you have to know that all things pass and perish,
and that what you've said is finite, but continue—
as if grand exceptions might be made—
raking the leaves, stacking the wood, hoping
the child falls asleep against your chest,
hoping the blizzard swerves, knowing the wreckage
of the present will be gathered but
not soon, and not by you, because you're in it,
there somewhere, under the sheet of snow.

The Theory of Everything

I.M. Karen Afton Lavers, 1956-2003
Donald William Lavers, 1945-2011

m

Before this, there was silence, just one
silence that had all these noises in it,
like those seven perfect seconds after lightning
where the static buzz and crackle
of what's coming boil. This was before
mass crumbled into *Kyrie, Gloria,*
Sanctus, Agnus Dei, before that nothingness
was shattered into all these somethings,
and before the space that made my body
different from yours, and therefore far away,
even when close. Those rifts let in the slow
hush of the snow, the blasted oak's white smoke,
that hum we hear inside of us, dark antimatter
gathering in everything like thunder.

Multiverse

The stars look infinite. But run the numbers:
they stop somewhere, and another universe
that holds ours in it like a Russian doll appears.

You're gone. How many faces, pale as yours,
will not open their eyes again, out there? Or worse,
are stacked inside you, like your coffin in this hearse?

Repeat, repeat, repeat, the sunlight whispers,
ramifying spacetime with our scars
and losses.
    But if everything occurs,
then somewhere past that, past black stars
and brilliant dark, you're holding pink bellflowers,

and we're sitting outside on some marble stairs
together, in the twilight, eating carmine pears—
still cold, and overripe, and almost ours.

=

The storm cloud's pent-up clamor
prattles on. It won't amount to much,
so ants resume dismantling their peach,
like math slowed down. The dusk rests like a rookery,
the rooks settle their font. I want a word that flies
like light, a constant that will carry
over upturned plots toward the sun,
something to whisper like a shibboleth
past sight into a better, if there is one,
state, no jot or tittle lost. A move that's more
than metaphor, before spring's foals become fall's flies
and float upstream. Before bodies combine
with time and turn to air: before that air
blooms in my body as this breath.

Credo

I thought your silence smoked me out
into the pointless pandemonium
of song and prayer, but your music is everywhere:
the well-fed fly, a fire eating air,
a swish of thistle, and the vultures' scrum,
a groaning whetstone, and the sighs
of earth taking a spade. Even the griefs that teethe
inside my bones and which you think are praise,
so multiply. Even the granite sky, the way my echoes
thrash me into unrequited dust.
I ache for Sabbath, Lord, some rest
from you, some pure caesura that could catch your breath,
or if you've filled my mouth, burn it of dross
until we both believe of silence *it was good*.

t

Milk River, 1979

Piled like clothes where the river bends,
summer ends. You won't return
until the high ice weeps into the bay,
except to gather more dead wood to burn.

The terns might come back like a tattered net,
infinities of hyacinths, embossed
inside a vast chainmail of frost,
might not survive the night, but either way

they will be waiting for you there next May,
and all the light you loved once will return
the fingertips that frost stole from the fern,

the blueberries that made the black bears stay,
the kingfisher still burning and still wet,
where you watched him, where the river ends.

Field Guide

Come little wind, come sad chinook, come catch
me like a weed, some strain of yellow vetch,
pluck nothing but the uncut rusty strings
of purple sedge and mouse-ear; strum these rows
of barberry and spread the milfoil's disease,
unsift the sleeping houndtongue and the toadflax,
drain the sour backwaters of my brain
to sow a line of henbane, tansy, ragwort,
brome, the greater groundsel then the lesser;
choke my ears with burs if you are there,
just speak as plainly as you can: say something,
true or not, like beargrass, not a grass,
which bears don't eat, no matter what it's called:
elk grass, turkey beard, quip quip, firelily.

Alberta Georgics

Of chinooks smooth-talking small infinities
of wheat; of tar-tanged topsoil,
and of fraying permafrost; of fire's falsetto

purifying pitch, and queasy bees
fading like smoke,
                              say something, Maro.
Scrape the frothy Tiber off your tongue,

its silty sighs, its golden gloss,
and tell me what might work up here.
The world's a wreck—forget poetry:

Speak to me stones you can say
when in Rome, but our wind won't
dictate, and our stones don't scribe.

·⑴llⅼ⑴·

Each silo bursts
                              its stanza, threshers
rake the stretch-marked hills, and dusk
stutters into dark more stars than sky.

Then light lands hard as wind,
pushing the sapling ash around,
late-blooming bog star and belated bur.

Our August might not awe its emperor.
But heavy kernels still salute and bow,
and plots the plow commissioned

are still crowned with gold, grainy vernacular:
Foeniculum vulgare,
                              ditch weed,
spiked with lice but spicing wind like licorice.

-ıllıı-

Great spectacle, in other words, neat furrows
and lush flocks. The problem's me:
the city boy arrives to clear his head,

thinking *the grey horse of the clouds,*
its half-apple of moon, but loses it:
the sky's immense miasma makes him sick.

A lavish fever, visitors, and dreams—
I've heard this one already, Maro—wisdom
spoken by a tatted, gap-toothed yokel

in a nonsense epilogue that twangs
like cricket song: *A dull plow cuts dull worms.*
Joy's like a fox: twenty-two pounds, but mostly fur.

-ıllıı-

But how unlikely, joy or grief,
or blades of grass, and how sufficient.
Fields catch flower overnight,

and then dissolve. Thistles exist,
and hawks are numerous, the taste
of soil more than we deserve,

the names of birds not a belated
plumage but distilled out of the wing,
woven of air; how startling

the silent sweep and pivot
of a word, and that the mind can feel
unfamiliar in the costume of itself.

The pumpjack hammers out its slick
hexameter. The truck whinnies exhaust.
Our work won't save us, since

the faintest breathing scars the sky.
So if you're sick of all that marble,
and would like to make cold granite weep,

if you crave empty fields where being,
steaming like a bull, can settle, come
and sing.
            I won't just do something,

I'll sit here. And I'll hold my breath,
and watch the dust your foot, keeping
the beat, kicks up, clouding the stars.

Linnaeus's Prayer

By the time of his death the Swedish botanist and zoologist, known as the "second Adam," had classified and named more than 4,400 species of animals and 7,700 species of plants.

thank you Lord for creations so numerous we have something to do with
    all these words

for words words enough to cull order from chaos sort flesh

forgive me for pressing flowers in books instead of boiling them down to
    make medicine

for lingering at streams for bowing to weeds

for naming us *Homo sapiens* after you wise being our echo our kin

for thinking your great work unfinished

vast dark crowded uncertain

but I have been faithful in my way

I do not write confessions or journals or poems about love

I do not express myself

there is too much to do the earth is still wild we must labor and sweat

give me words that ensure what exists will survive

and words that will grant life to swamps deserts moldering bones

take under your protection Carl Elisabeth Sophia Lovisa Sara Johannes and
    small Magdalena

and those who departed too soon without tasting air

without being named

teach me to speak so that they will rise and greet us

that we may dwell on the banks of the great delta

where all creatures gather

to be called forth and known and made whole

that this work might continue *in excelsis* forever amen

Cryptozoologist

It snorted, coyly close, if that's the word,
defunct by its own breathing, mortified
I think by me, but condescending to be
seen the way one sees a silhouette,
like when leaves fall onto a lake and drape
the sand below in leopard-printed shade.
No bigger than itself, with height and width,
and moths that haloed it like purple steam.
Eyes, but not exactly. Ears, if I'd addressed them.
Not brash, not timid, almost like a dying
to exist, a hope I loathed for letting
me conceive it. It was not what it was—
an angry consonant I'd hurled to break
like crockery against the canyon wall.
Or else the humming of the Byrd *Te Deum*
heard through vestry marble. But more than that
I couldn't say. I thought that I should praise it
for some reason, but it wandered off,
brushing out its footprints as it went,
and leaving nothing but a thing-shaped hole
behind it in the air, as if pushed off the edge
of being, but neither to fly or fall. Whereas I
couldn't move. Not even to raise my camera.

Elegy

While that sheep staggered
up the gravel road, stooped low,
unsheathing seablush from the dirt,
and through a skin of August snow,

or after, when a whisper
warmed the horsetail and heal-all,
wooing the cows, panning an empire
of reeds for one last pastoral?

While wind plucked everlasting,
miles away in shoaling light
your last words, like a harp string,
snapped: *don't be afraid,* you said, and died.

Don't be afraid, you said, and died
like everybody else, your first cliché.
But day does turn to night,
fallow to seed, hayseed to hay.

Of course you died. But why
should I try stitching wounded air
with breath where yours should ramify
the bloodroot, foxglove, toad's prayer?

Shepherds plaiting phlox and lily,
filigreeing with their sighs
your vacancy, cannot buck gravity,
or sweet-talk ice, or cauterize

the wind. They loiter and award
prizes for mourning, string a fence
of syllables around their herd
as if claiming the place grief ends,

language begins. They sing all night.
And so, as when a yearling, spooked,
believes its mother might
be there, I turned and looked.

You weren't. Upstream,
the bees spit out another hive,
and the she-goat's twins steam,
inconceivably alive.

The Suicide Angels

Like poppies bending down
to clear their heads of rain—

too swayed by emptiness
to rise again—

some lay, heavy
with reasons, on our lawns,

some washed up on our shores
like sad sea cows.

Maybe they'd traced perfection
to its edge

and jumped, hoping
to trade

the Church of the Everlasting
for the Church of the Fleeting

and Plain.
In time, and as if stoned

on gravity, they rose,
smelling like burnt perfume,

all bright like soil after rain,
all darkly bruised.

Assure us, we said, others
remained happy

to mourn you;
that those you left do not miss

temporal form,
or that perfection too

has its material.
Tell us such bliss, for most,

is bearable,
that we can hoist the burden

of a happiness
without variety or end.

But they had not come back
to comfort us.

They simply moaned
like struck bells

when we shook them,
and then walked away, leaving

their greasy prints like thieves
on everything—the skylights

and the pears, the mirrors
and the decorative spoons.

The Task

At least once, let us try to approach the center of the real problems.

I mean the real ones.

Such as why, when you did not ask to be made, we insisted.

As if you will never taste evil, dear child, and know only the grass, the way it sags just before cutting, thick and heavy with dew.

As if that much sufficed.

No—we walk on the roof of Hell, the boards are brittle and thin.

Not only thin, but missing in patches. Suffering flickers, unceasingly there.

You will be tempted to seek your revenge on the world, or demand consolation, or believe that it's all a mistake—that you belong somewhere else:

a city of green leaves, light wind, stars watching us greedily. A stable horizon. All things known.

But rejoice: we are here. So we stand. We go into it, a place which eludes description: good days, bad days, days drifting like smoke through our ravenous arms.

I hold you, but only as much as the sea holds the hull of a ship: always lapping against it, and never discerning much more than an outline, a bright mass with somewhere much farther to go.

Some sea will lie always between us.

Rain falls, and I can hardly believe it.

I promise you, this is not poetry.

A luminous wind fills the mountains and valleys, melting the high snow, and stoking the aspen like pillars of fire.

The swaying maples creak and snore. A blithe hawk doodles on air.

We have so little time.

I don't know if you'll find me again at the end, if there is one, or how soon you'll get to lie down.

All I know is your task is immeasurably great. It cannot be accomplished, yet it cannot be avoided:

persist, little heart. Straighten up, shoulders. Move, legs. Go forward. Bear yourself over the ruinous world.

Will Exult over You with Loud Singing

That's my dad, I say, pointing to the man in the photograph
with thin grey hair reflecting river-light.
And that's my mom. My arch of nose, my chin.

I'm talking to my children, talking the way I do
about things that are not lost, that are still here,

knowing that it's no use, that time and decay
do not obey language; that the dumb flesh of a tree,
for instance, doesn't care about Samantha,
which word my son, ten years from now,

will carve into it;

doesn't distinguish between the pain of his love for her,
and any old pain: woodpecker, beetle, axe, frost, flame.

·‖‖·

Once, when I said she could not play
with a dead mouse, my daughter wailed so loud

I thought she might break.

This was in Great Falls, next to a riverbank
wafted with small blue moths. We'd strayed
from the playground near an overpass where people
seemed to be sleeping or hovering around fires.

She yelled *Mine,* astounding even herself, as if at the end
of the scream she thought there might be nothing left,

nothing of her,
nothing to listen to in this world.

The sad mechanic exercise...
—Tennyson

My mother was finishing a master's degree
in psychiatric nursing, writing a thesis
on gambling addiction, on people who wear diapers
so they can stay at slot machines for hours,
even days,

and when we asked her if we should try
to get the last course waived and the degree granted
before it was too late, she said nothing,
as if keeping new and hidden counsel
with herself, or with someone not present.

And my father,
dead ten years later of a heart attack
in the bathroom of a movie theatre—the ticket-taker

panting out that sad mechanic CPR—he must have felt
a terrible silence growing inside him, or a noise
too loud to hear, the crashing stillness after
a long inertia, the indifference
of that small wet machine suddenly reluctant to bear

for one more second

the weight of his body. As if the soul

at the end of a long journey
finally stepped through a door and put down its luggage.

Thinking, maybe, if he listened hard enough
he could make out
why stars had lost their willingness to dazzle,
or where they were going—through what dark nimbus
or invisible crack—and why without him,

why so fast.

·ıllıı·

Once as a child I drove a hammer's claw into
the trunk of one of the small maples
lining our driveway,

peeling bark away in strips as thick as fingers
to the underflesh, the soft wet honey-gold,
tinted a bit off-pink, off-green.

It was like being, or imagining that I could be,
everywhere at once, light
right there in the palm of my hand,
made still and, well,

mine.

In ruins. Light's unsingable psalm,
a thing outside
our frail economy of come and go.

A brief end to stagnation, briefly glimpsed.

My father was angry, but mostly bewildered.
He stared for a while, then said only
that the hammer wasn't mine to take, and that the tree
wasn't mine to do whatever I thought I was doing to it.
And what are you doing to it, he said, and I said

I don't know.

·⑾·

Poor flesh, love says, bearing her teeth.
Poor agitation of heat, of stars, shaking and far away.

Van Gogh in the final letter to his brother Theo:

Well, my own work,
I am risking my life for it and my reason
has half foundered because of it—that's all right.

It's true no metaphor can save us, store us
like gravel in the cheek of Hallelujah Creek,

Creek of Unclottable Light.
But that's alright.

Why not exist, at least for each other,
in love and thickly streaked and made to end,
believing, if not everything, at least
one of the minor prophets, maybe,

Zephaniah: *he will rejoice over you with gladness;*
he will quiet you by his love;
he will exult over you with loud singing.

⫸⫷

That's my mom I say to my kids,
that look she has like mine, of somebody enduring
happiness, expecting grief. *And that,* I say,

is her diploma, framed and hanging on the wall.

This is your breakfast, bananas and toast and jam,
our one life, ours in the only sense
that matters, something that we make ... make what?

Come forth, I think,

like stars, all flicker and distance, prodigal and dim,
but not so dim that if they vanished

we would not weep every night,
or stop trying—though we knew we couldn't—
to describe them.
                              To remember.

A Prophet

Drinking the dregs of my despair,
I dragged across a wilderness
and met a six-winged seraph where
two roads converted to a cross.
Lightly as sleep, he touched my eyes,
glutting them on prophesies
until, insatiable, they looked
up like a fledgling eagle's, spooked.
Without speaking he filled my ears
with the shudderings of spheres,
and sullen mumblings of heaven,
the bursting of each bud and vine,
the sudden thump of brooding wings,
invisible reptilian seethings
underwater. Then he seized
my tongue, still writhing and diseased
with guile, and with a blood-
stained hand he severed it and sewed
a snake's slick fork onto the root.
He split open my chest, cut out
my heart, then stooped to cauterize
the black wound with live coal. God's voice
called me as I woke on the sand,
strewn like a corpse: *Stand*
up, Prophet; speak, and I will fill
your mouth with my unbending will:
hold my Word's torch to every town,
to every heart, and burn them down.

from Pushkin

The Great Web

A world in which a better one can be dreamed of is not the worst.
—Julien de Valckenaere

The message came at night, melting the snow,
spooking the dogs, and hushing shadows with the news
that we need not fear suffering or death,
that these were part of something called
The Great Web, and that all would be well.
That sounded right, we thought. It would explain
not just the guns, or floods, or fires, or plagues,
or hurricanes, or wars, but all the meetings
we'd been stuck in, and the traffic,
and the piles of dirty dishes, since
they too had purposes ordained from the beginning,
and would end. It would explain the darkness,
and suggest a better light was on its way
and would unfurl secret spectrums
in the soapy water like a paper fan. It would
explain the boy, the reasons he was living
on the street, that what we saw as ravings
were dictated by a doting angel
or a tender muse. And it would tell us
how that woman from the tenth floor fell,
her orange dress unfurling like a flame
around her through the breathless air.
It meant that any second she'd get up again,
and tie her hair behind her, wipe the mud
off of her face, pick up her shoes,
and never once look up, and walk away.

Patmos Revisited

No green clouds hang like a divine disease,
no hot breath haunts the back of the neck,
no claws clink their dictation across shale.
Oyster-shell sand still scatters the light, but songs
the sea murmurs seem scum-fringed, colloquial,
their rhythms private and indifferent
to us; no tides of purple crabs rising
through town, bearing the dead back down to sea.
And dreams, when they happen now, are dreams:
we bore each other with them over breakfast.
No sun's blunt fist, no bruise of earth; instead,
leaf-colored leaves, and cow-faced cows,
and nameless toads that spook us while we sleep;
a perfect darkness making shadows disappear,
nights punctuated by someone downshore,
braining an octopus against a stone.

Prospero in Milan

. . . where
Every third thought shall be my grave.

The Earth turns in its sleep. My palace sleeps,
my servants sleep and dream. Miranda crown'd
in Naples sleeps with belly round and kicking
like a wave-filled globe. I only under heaven
cannot conjure rest, and wander moonlit
streets slipper'd and pantaloon'd, pregnant
with dreams that cannot get born, a duke
by title but with power to command
only the gardener, and to coax from earth
no demi-puppets now but dew-drunk snails.

I who pull'd leviathans from briny
beds on hooks of nothing, of words, taut air,
and with sweet sounds made them to gambol ewe-like
on the sand; who made stars fall and caus'd
eclipses of the sun and moon, am now
too powerless even to die, and envy
what the sailors and their drabs, the pimply
love-besotted youths, the poppy-monger
in his smoky bed, his mouth agape,
achieve with ease: forgetfulness and dream,
that final dream whose smoke consumes the dreamer,
banish'd from his breath to no isle known.

Is there some task or spell remaining? Or
has Prospero not prosper'd? No rest earn'd?
As toads inhale strength from vapors in a bog
so I gain'd power plotting my revenge,
for titles taken and for strength abjur'd,

and yielded to no good dullness then.
Having at last my dukedom got my thoughts
unclench'd to mercy, sweet oblivion,
to steaming loam and the decay of things.
But now I wait, and hear court news, and yawn,
remembering like fragments of a dream
a life more rich in its adversity
than all this kingdom's peace and pomp: the island
and its bright green rain, the misty fens
where tall bee-heavy flowers bloom'd, the night-flies
that would plague my daughter's sleep until
I learned what vegetable infusions, drugs
and minerals, what mandrake root and wormwood
salves could keep them back; the promontories
and the standing pools where living shadows
throng'd to do my bidding; caves and brooks
and glens and fields and bogs, the smash'd and shining
tablet of the sea whose mermaids sang to soothe
my child's fears and calm my salt-rack'd brain.

Now no one sings.
And Ariel is gone, beyond the wind.
And Caliban, who loved me, whom I nursed
from an abhorrent babe into an almost man,
on whom so many human pains were wasted,
nightly tears, which never have run dry,
he, ingrate, now forgets his language, bows
to strange gods on the hard rocks, cursed to be
as free as any under the punishing sun.

Or he is dead, and luckier than me,
who sits and reads beside a garden wall

i' th' afternoon, swollen with sighs, waiting
for sleep. I hear the rumors of some distant
storm disturb the windchimes, as if gathering
to take me back, afraid some days I should
have never left, afraid I am the island
and will never die. I sing old songs,
and watch my snails, drenched with dew, bowing
their drowsy horns to greet me of a morning,
trailing glad slime everywhere. I drop them
lettuce, cowslips, cabbage, musk-rose, fig,
pink honeysuckle, but am otherwise
a deaf indifferent god to such as these.

I must learn how to die or I am not
myself, untender and insensible.
The Earth must let me go or the abysmal sea
will take me back and give me now a glimpse
of that dark world, whose powers bid me trade
a grave of dirt for that unfathom'd nook
where curious fish right now peruse my book,
and oozy sea-winds fondle an immortal page.

How to Die, and When

Like learning how to shoot, you have to practice,
practice holding still, then stiller, still
enough to tell the noise of wind in white pine
from the noise of wind in red. You have
to breathe through your whole body, like the sea,
and slowly, until you're all exhalation,
and then sky. You have to visualize—
yes life is long, spiders exist, and yes
you're forced to sweat, and bleed, and smile,
and pretend you're not already smoke
inside, and ash, and blown away, and yes,
on top of that, you have to keep walking
the dog, and making food, and cleaning up,
and not just once, or once a day, but all day,
and for years. But push all that away.
Those images aren't what will help you now.
Instead, picture a boat. You see the fish scales
smeared along the seat, the backup oar,
the man steering the outboard, fiddling
his beard? You see the dock you left from shrink,
and duck under the clouds, and disappear?
Then it's already over. It's too late.
The trigger finger and the heart have waited
years for this, and can't be stopped.
The breeze has settled. Here's your window. Go.

And Then a Little Nothingness Was Measured at the Galaxy's Core

Not wings beating in purposeful and never-ending flight; no wave that cradled us, keeping the stars apart.

Just nothing, filling up space, coming for us: the thought that if we were not needed at the center, light-years over there, then we weren't needed here. It left nothing to claw at, nothing to dig. The hopes with which we'd comforted each other yesterday all gone, the old assurances, the surface wonders and the central beams.

And so we wept, until the emptiness vibrated, and a few small trees appeared, or reappeared, much changed, their new, naked gesticulations reimagined bit by bit into a kind of bloom.

We dug our children out of nothing, children who had no idea why we were looking at them differently and thinking You are my bright world.

Slowly the fields and wetlands were recovered, and the swans that wander them, a little frayed and tarnished, but aglow.

All this was years ago. Our sleep, mostly, is back. Churches are full. But still patches of nothing catch us unaware. Go down a gravel road, and there it is, holding its ground: no wind, no stars, no clouds.

Whole chapters of Stendhal or Thackeray no one remembers. And the reasons that you pull the weeds from the tomato beds, or clean the eaves out, or enjoy watching the swallows swoop and veer still sometimes disappear.

The chalk you used to bang from the erasers in the schoolyard as a kid, where did it go?—the way it drifted through the air, into the trees, over the snow.

Eclogue Hidden in the Trunk of a Tree

We are heading to the border on foot
with our son who is very ill, pausing only
to write this note to you and hide it here
in this dark wood, the spot agreed upon,
uncertain if you will receive it. Guards
patrol the mountains, and always now
there is the smell of smoke, and winds rise up
bringing the black leaves off the trees in sheets,
a sound like the tearing of paper. Last night
the bits of quartz that caught the moonlight
blinked this warning to me as we walked:
Turn back. They're waiting for you up ahead.
The world might seem to hover on the cusp
of clarity, it might appear that new
transmissions will start creeping through the chaos
any day, a harmony that will reveal things,
transcendent things. But no: the universe
has long outlived its usefulness. This is the end.
I pass this message on to you, and then
must go: the dark gesticulating willows
know where we are hiding, and conspire
in semaphore. The time may come when we
will see each other, but until we do,
beware: the stars, the roads, the swaying weeds,
the white geese bathing in a brackish pond—
all things conceal and are not what they seem.
The clouds may look like clouds, but don't
forget our enemies control the wind. In rain
and spreading shadows they slink through the world.

The New Arrivals

There was a crowd there, waiting. Everybody
stared, the way you do your first day
in a strange place. And the sun was up now,
and the last stray stars of Capricorn had fled.
One of the new arrivals looked at us and said:
"Please tell us, if you know, which of these paths
leads to the mountain." And my guide responded,
"you think we belong here, that we know
this place. We don't. We're strangers too.
We also just arrived, just barely before you,
but by another way, a way so steep and rough
that this new climb will feel like rest."
But they'd already paled: they had noticed
I was breathing, that I had a body, that I lived.
Like when a messenger, holding an olive branch,
brings news some far-flung town has longed for,
and gets sighted from the gate, and thronged,
that's how they crowded me, as if forgetting
they were dead already, and that now the only thing
they had to do was go, and become beautiful.

Purgatorio, canto II, lines 52-75

How to Be Dead

You can forget the body, since it soon grows cold.
Much harder to forget your name, holding
its warmth inside it like a coral sea.

Forget the light. Even the loam there shines,
and faces shine, and shade. Forget the moon,
because instead, a steady moan of sharp wings

wrings from you a thick harvest of praise,
a sound like flies drowning in honey,
perfection stiff as mud frozen in snow.

Forget the snow. The crude prelude of days
you leave behind dissolves like dross, or chaff
winnowed from rows of wheat. Forget those too.

All our apostrophes to snuffed-out stars
might part the smoke and chorus you, well-dressed,
through rarer air. But first, you can't forget

to kick yourself clear of our atmosphere,
slick gravity, this rash of sun, past flesh
and blood, freed from the orbit of their need.

When we put the hymnals down, corral
our vowels inside consonants, fence in our griefs,
you'll still be dead. The dead survive

outside our sentences, past songs, and after Earth,
beyond the burnt-sap smell of March, the bloodmoon
of November, the haymaking of June.

Letter from Deep Space

The view's not much.
Sometimes faint constellations
sweep like crows.
But mostly shadows,
almost the color of lily pads
deep under water.

No sound; not even
wavelengths of white noise
writhing like eels
in a satellite's net.

I miss the dead flies
that littered the sills
of windows on Earth.

The distance to nothingness
used to be infinite:
dusk and a stray dog
chasing down stars.
Can you hear me? I'm shooting
at houseflies with cannons—
words fall back to Earth:

There were so many trees there
that a squirrel could cross two thousand miles
—from Tyumen to Irkutsk—
without touching the ground.

Light Years

Mostly the desire to feed themselves,
and the rusty lineage of tools invented
to that end. Everything else was waiting,
discussions about weather interrupted
only by the need to bury their dead.
They tried their hardest to kill time, to fill
the gaps left open by survival. Wars helped.
And so did painting, from what we can tell.
At thirty-two feet per second per second, children
fell into the dirt, were cleaned, and given names.
Birds that left in fall came back in spring.
Churches were interred in coats of moss,
the doctors washed their hands, and viruses
made promises to blood that nobody
could break. They cried out hoping
someone heard; they spoke in darkness,
but the darkness grew. They called it life,
but we don't know what it was for. We only
know that they were brief, and somewhere
over there, beyond those stars, light years ago.

Meeting of Exiles

And setting up from shore,
my ships settled at anchor there, I saw,
by chance, in a green grove by the city gate,
beside streams shining like Simois back home,
Andromache, doomed queen! giving to dust
libations, petitions, prayers, all proper rites
of grief, beseeching Hector's ghost to come
and consecrate the place her heartache crowned
and hallowed like a tomb: twin altars of turf,
an asylum of shade where she could shed her tears.

Beholding me, and my barrage of men
bedecked in Troy's regalia, she shook,
astonished, and, fearful of omens, fell.

Some minutes passed before her swoon subsided
and she spoke: "what's this? Are you alive?
Are you a true form, with a living face,
bringing one more bad message, Goddess-born?
Or if life's light has leaked from you and you
are shade, say something of my slaughtered Hector.
Tell me where he is," her weeping filling
the grove, and me, with her great anguish.

So I began, saying in broken gasping
phrases: "don't fear. I'm alive, still moving
through misfortune's merciless maze.
But what has happened to you, bereft of husband?
Could any life make up for such a loss?
Are you still wed to Pyrrhus, wife and slave?"

To which she whispered, with her head weighed down:
"I envy even Priam's daughter, lucky enough
to die at Troy's tall walls, entombed with enemies,
not cursed like us to keep on living, cast
by Greek lots into Greek beds, bound
in mock marriage to conquering masters.
Our city racked, we were raised from the ruins
and sent across various seas, myself a servant
to Achilles' son, bearing in bondage
heirs for him until he met Hermione
and gave me Helenus as husband, slave
espoused to slave. It's a long story.
Orestes murdered Pyrrhus and parts of Pyrrhus'
kingdom were conferred to Helenus,
who has regained, in part, the paradise
we knew, tall Trojan-style towers, Trojan walls.

But what about you? What winds or wars
conspired to cast you on our coastline?
What of your boy, Ascanius? Alive?
Tasting the air? Even in burning Troy
I thought...but no.
Does he remember his mother? How much
of the old spirit survives, the old strength?
How much of what men stood for still remains?"

Aeneid, Book III, lines 300-343

Invective against Stars

What could the stars have, in their burnt perfection,
that we don't? They shine, but just enough
to make the darkness visible. They guide,
but they themselves seem lost, moving in circles
over spacetime's swaying, night-blue sea.
Behind the house it is the moon that swaths
the tiger lilies in a pinkish grey,
the moon that soothes the berries' sunburned flesh,
the moon that shows a single spruce bough dipping
where an owl was. What do the stars know
of the momentary, of this moment,
when the funeral is over, and the dinner
dishes cleared away, and you're outside,
tasting the pleasures of another breath
you know will end, and soon, and you look up,
and there they are, hopelessly beautiful?
Come back inside. There's nothing up there for you.
Just let them have their sorry lingering.
And let them wallow in their hoarded years.
What we have are those evenings when
disarray is gathered and pressed to the chest:
deft stumbles, furrows of grace, ice in the glass,
an open window letting cool air in,
a little breeze, a little moth-flecked breeze . . .

The Rustle of Hemlock

I don't know what I'm supposed to want
from this, my stagnant sea of days,
the endless hours I must part with
breath and breath and breath, or else
be silent in, and drown, these nights,
when lost thoughts rise as flotsam
to the surface of the mind and scrape
the inside of my skull; the hours of granite
and the hours of ash, the dark light-year,
the spark that shattered it, the signature
of smoke it scribbled through singed air.
Each day redoes the vast undoing
of the last. What's in between are dreams,
more shadows, snow falling on snow,
a boy leading a tame bear on a leash
along a ditch, an empty silo on a distant hill,
the cracked, off-key sonata of the moon
whose gauzy cadences could make one fall
in love with dust and madness and despair,
the soil tinged pink from wars upstream,
a river on whose currents, as if from my arms,
the last few leaves slip silently away.

That to Philosophize Is to Learn to Die

I have been glad to live, philosophers.
I have been glad.
        I have been glad to weep,
to praise a world all gauzed and vanishing:
       I am alive, this is the air,
that is the glorious sun, there are the skaters,
trailing thick wool scarves behind them in the wind.

I've praised the wind, Pythagoras,
              the way
it drags the baying of the dogs into my sleep.
The world is that which passes, or has past,
and I am glad.
       And I am glad, Maimonides,
and I am glad, John Stuart Mill:
the jays are blue,
         Being is good, things want
to appear, and I am here simply to see

the forms they step forth in, the waves they surface
as:
      red cedar, cinnamon, white alder, teak,
Letters to Theo, and the Champs-Elysées.

How lucky, Heraclitus, to consider, "to create
a self where there was none, how right

to assert yourself, how right to feel desire,"
to whisper to your life
         you are not lost,
your days are here, their cold bearable sway

drifting and spare, like snow that came
while you were sleeping, laying little blankets
on the cows. And I am glad.

                              If I could say
What does it matter that this bliss will end?

What does it matter, Leibniz, in a world
like this—
                    Claire's blouse still damp
in places from her bath, the baby finally asleep—

if he is on his way right now, strolling
those hills?
                    What then, Lao-Tzu?
What would become of my desire for coffee,
or for lemon grated into sticky dough,

or to the pleasures of arranging things as I
and *not-I*?
                    Or of rearranging them,
bringing the warm cup to my mouth, or Claire
into my jittery, impatient arms?

My voice is hoarse, Marcus Aurelius,
and I am glad.
                    "I am glad"—even to say that much
is difficult, dear Simone Weil,
                              and gladness passes on
              over an empty fleeting outer world—

but don't cry, Derrida; don't worry, Nietzsche:
who speaks lives, and what is said endures.

Dawn like a sieve, dusk like a shattered jar,
clouds like grey whale calves, fattened on light.

"Since there's no help, come let us kiss and part . . ."
And I am glad, Descartes . . .

                and I am glad, Camus . . .

And I am glad, and I am glad.

There has been fish covered in coarse Greek salt.
There are these jays. There are

                those dusk-bruised hills.

Works and Days

       Light, so heavy Earth groaned like a boat,
the horsemint, milkweed, sorrel, vetch,
red gorse and pink marsh vapors that dissolve
coarse clouds and without losing breath bloody
the moon; a yellow house, a flock of goats
who feed on ruin and wail and will not spook;
the silver grass around the lake, and angels,
falling just to feel fall's cadences:
       I want to say whatever's missing,
here it is, inside this wind that's reached
the cypress bough outside your window,
waking you. That's all it was. I'm here
now, and will stay a while, and then morning
will come. We'll try *The Earth is like unto*
a parable: for those with ears to hear;
and, Nature's not a shambles; and, as your mother
put it once, while whipping cream: *Life*
will be appreciated, or else; my prodigal
accountings of chronologies which now
belong to me, too soon unsponsored, and to you,
too soon their little heirs, this hope to save you,
if not all, then, something. First things.
Patch work. Before the rains begin:
       In the beginning there was silver grass
around the lake where she who made all this
built up a house, and multiplied her flock.
He pointed up at her and she said *Moving water;*
then he pointed to himself: she said *Mooncalf.* He grew
and made small horses do big things and planted
when the stars, he thought, so clearly said
plant now. But knapweed.
              Hawkweed.

Medusahead.
                Thistle, marsh.
                              Thistle, plumeless.
Loostrife, goatgrass, buckthorn, dyer's woad
are not the consequences of some ancient curse:
they're things, and things are always growing
harder to explain. Man comes and tills the field
and lies beneath. Sometimes fantastic
effort simply fails. We live and die and think
there was a day before this sour air, a time
when angels hovered, thick as cowbirds on an ox.
But Earth was never better than it is right now.
Each winter juncos bend their song to dearth,
the Earth's, I think, best rhyme.
Then lynx tracks annotate the trail behind you
where, just now, blank snow. A box of oranges,
still faintly green. And sixty four species of birch.
What is Olympus if it can vanish in a cloud,
or Eden if its fences are so small?

·illi·

                    Autumn was here first;
the yellow leaves do not need your approval.
You're not obliged to sorrow, or to joy,
but in seasons of joy, be absolute;
in sorrow, weep, and be not comforted.
Some proof demand of heaven, but not much;
the acres where Seth was conceived, and where,
feeling he had a special claim, he jawboned
William to the ground. Then there was Mary,

five years old, who screamed from unknown pain,
for seven days, until she died. The Earth is full
of evil things; the sky, full of the vultures'
patient whorls. So they dug a hole
and buried her and went to bed. And then
got up again. For what? Coffee and milk
and a nice quince jam? What is the best thing?
An apple? Fresh saskatoons?
That's how easily we are seduced:
a six-month winter, but the first loose scab
of ice, the first card-table dragged outside
for brunch, stippled in honey, and we're sure
the world's always like this, flaunting
its gaudy maples like new money.
Lynx tracks on the trail right behind you;
light, nothing and everything at once,
that color where greenfinches end
and goldfinches begin.
                    And Seth gathered anew.
And the Lord filled all his granaries, and cattle
well-stricken in age were multiplied:
While earth remaineth, seedtime and harvest,
and cold and heat, and summer and winter,
and day and night shall not cease.
That was their promise. It wasn't meant for us.
Too many things and not enough forms,
and so we drift. The wind won't turn the torn rags
of our bodies into sails. The milk pail of the galaxy
has spilled; the willows bend and break
and drape their heavy clothes onto the stones.
Days bend and shed their sunlight like a skin,
while into pitiless darkness frays the moon.

Somebody wasn't buried fast enough.
Or somebody was kissed, and the sewers
of some vermin's veins, finer than Rome's,
invaded ours until even the hawkweed
shivered in aftershock. Miles of silver birch
unraveled atmospheres of gauze
but couldn't staunch the rheumy, rife,
and restless air. Distance, that old god,
was dead. How can we think of thinking
to explain? *The world is that which happens
to be the case?* Better a love of shaping soil,
upturned rows well-tamped, before time
stops to catch its breath, set down its spade,
and scrape its boots of you; small order, finish,
straightness realized; harvests of sweat
and sound perfection, absolute
control over a practiced hand that can exactly
hover like an osprey in a sunspot's sliver,
stilled inside the faddish current
of hot air by vast fine-tunings
of its feathers' flickering, or fold,
and fall, gutting the salmon-colored air,
a limitless dominion
over small but salvageable fields.
The bees grow louder right before a frost.
Better some botched opus than a perfect silence.
Better a century of creaking floors
and carpet she capitulated to
to cover bloodstains and the smell

of afterbirth the hardwood exhaled
in hot sun; better, even, the goat
army that sacked it, breeding on the beds,
eating the wallpaper, the glue,
the curtains, Shreve's dress uniform,
the roses, and ten inches of topsoil,
than blank fields. Better the lurid steaming
of the windfall plums, the hatchling tensure
when the foaming mooneye bites,
the blood's curt countercoil and—enough:
fewer adjectives, more nouns. *Serein:* a fine rain
falling after sunset from a sky in which
no clouds are visible. *Serac:* a ridge of ice crowning
the surface of a glacier. Ants queueing
to higher ground, the prairie sounding charlock,
rapeseed, Job's tears, milkweed, sorrel—
quick, before everything goes, let's put them
in our little book: the fireweed, the wood lily,
the whispering of snow.

·◂|||▸·

I'd yield everything and live well on a line or two
of winter sedge, the mare's saltlick, a muddy spring
where some slim muse would say *Fatten your sheep,
and then be silent!* But your birthright
will not be abridged: abundance also
fell under our stewardship. And joy.
Ann made a dress, a white pine was a witness,
and what rings they had

spread from a rising trout. Granaries, half-built, rose
no further, and the wheat fermented into
fumes that made even the mayflies dizzy.
We were the only yield that year, the ears
a honeymoon's hexameter conceived.
Whom would their temperance
have pleased? Remember
all the silver grass around the lake?
All kinds of things exist. Why shouldn't we
be happier? . . . *a world which though wicked
enough in all conscience is* perhaps *as good
as worlds unknown* is tempting, I agree,
but no. Salvation from our smoking detritus
in clichés of *a better world?*
Unsatisfactory. The end must be
to cultivate perpetual astonishment
right now, and watch light bail
darkness from the flooding sky.
Earth's earth. The rest is silence,
and I've had enough of that already.
Gods, and Mooncalf naming grasses
by the sound they made in wind, then Shreve,
Mary, five Wills in a row, then Beulah,
then the quack touch Doctor who preached
mostly Babylon, and knew the resting place
of Noah's ark, the names of all the priests
of Baal; and then Lord Al, of nothing
that we knew, and all *nomina dubia*
the night will swallow in its senseless sea.
*Do not the chaste lines of this ark
deny the dominion of space?* It doesn't matter—
just keep going: Afton, mom, me, you,

the little center of this crumbling chiasmus,
you, me, mom, and Afton, who filled
fifteen black folios with clippings:
brown blue-ribbon calves, the nurses' strike,
fat birth announcements, lean obituaries,
Sarajevo, Munich, D-Day; each faded
photograph a little grave of light.

·ᴵᴵᴵᴵᴵ·

When the moon threatens to jump if you don't heed it,
keep your head down, hoe your acre, think
this is the row I will consider now. This one,
no other. And yet, aim at no less than all the world.
Mooncalf lay with Beulah. Elizabeth
bore twins so early they were kept in bread pans
in the oven for a week. That happened—
not just another of my indolent exaggerations—
in the season of blue damselflies, when all
the violet saxifrage was still in bloom,
and swaths of wapiti browsed the mustard fields
and diamond willows courted, coiffed in crows.
This had something to do with soothing you,
and calling, with dumb songs, your nightmare's bluff,
with turning fear into some air that can unravel
wind before it tears more genera
out of the tree of life, and you wake up
to ravaged, famished versions of reality.
What about *I did not, however, commit*
suicide because I wanted to know more
about mathematics. Too academic?

The beauty of literature: I lose a cow,
I write about its death, and this brings me
in enough to buy another cow. Too literal?
It should have been impossible not to love
all things in a world so filled . . . I cannot
make it any clearer: there were
lynx tracks on the trail right behind me.
Too many things and not enough forms.
Not to *add to the stock of available*
reality but rather to *describe existence*
and convince ourselves to it, to walk
the field's length, and then walk back. Repeat.
It's simple, but I've lost my way.
Sixty-four species of birch. Fresh saskatoons,
the strings of bees that sow the wild rye west,
Heaven and Earth, what else? Commit it all
to memory: the silver grass
around the lake, the hole in snow
from which a thin umbilical of breath
upcoiled from the bear's enormous sleep,
that uncle throwing Hesiod in the fire—
First the Tower of Babel, and now this.
What could I learn from someone
who spells labour with no u. Barbarians, your poets.
All connoisseurs of shade. Shepherds
Plowmen, dead canoeists. Who?
It doesn't matter,

                    they're just names,
sweet prince, sweet
                  lady, sound and smoke,
and veiling anything we try to hold.
Every summer has a thousand hours

of light, so heavy, Earth groans like a boat,
but that much falls in one Venusian day.
The world seems all behind us but
might not be. Let's turn and look:
the cows will soon be up, staining their
jabots in green drool. The violet
saxifrage will bloom, and dawn will come.

⋅⋅⫯⫯⫯⋅⋅

And dawn will come, carrying its dish of milk
with both hands over the hills. That is
enough. I will get up again. I will make
eggs. How can I justify despair at this,
when bats illumine air by whispering,
and she-wolves polish their blind cubs
until they shine? Let's not wrong Earth
a second time by bungling the elegy.
Dogwood, soapweed, bergamot, cinquefoil,
August hay still steaming under January snow,
red gorse, pink vetch, blue damselfly,
a box of oranges, still slightly green,
and Afton's commonplace, the goat army's
mad pica, all the boot eaters,
polygamists and prophets, unversed,
gods from out-of-county, shattering
the snowpack, pausing here to bury
frostbit grain like loot until new generations
grafted with the city's stock; all so-called
baser matter, with your quiet
wonder, each time, at the quiet moon.

A miniscule calamity of words
to wrap around us at the very end.
Two deer were eating millet near the lake;
I pointed and said *Look* . . . But you
weren't even there.

                    Man comes
and tills the field
                 and lies beneath.
In the beginning, silver grass around the lake.
I'm here now, and will stay a while,
and then morning will come.
                        Rest,
crow. Rest, dove. Rest, rest.
                       And so she wept,
and knelt down, kissing the earth,
saying *Here is a good land: a little*
clover, and a little sedge; here I will build
a great house, and till fields where my goats
can multiply, carving the future plot
in creek sand with her foot. And this is all
that's left. It's all I know.

Acknowledgments

Grateful acknowledgement is made to the editors of journals in which versions of these poems appeared:

AGNI Online	"Field Work"
Alaska Quarterly Review	"On Water, in Childhood"
Antioch Review	"Invective against Stars"
Baltimore Review	"Light Years"
Beloit Poetry Journal	"Works and Days"
Best New Poets 2015	"Patmos Revisited"
The Columbia Review	"A Prophet"
Crazyhorse	"m"
	"="
	"Field Guide"
elsewhere	"Linnaeus' Prayer"
Epoch	"Alberta Psalm"
Georgia Review	"Abridged Taxonomy of Light"
Hotel Amerika	"The Great Web"
Measure	"t"
Michigan Quarterly Review	"How to Die, and When"
New Ohio Review	"The Burden of Humans"
Rattle	"Coda"
	"Will Exult Over You with Loud Singing"
River Styx	"Elegy"
Saranac Review	"Credo"
Smartish Pace	"Andromache's Lullaby"
Southwest Review	"How to Be Dead"
	"The Invention of Birds"
Tampa Review	"Cosmography"
	"Eclogue Hidden in the Trunk of a Tree"
	"The Task"
	"The New Arrivals"
	"The Suicide Angels"
	"The Rustle of Hemlock"
	"Letter from Deep Space"

TriQuarterly	"Alberta Georgics"
West Branch	"Instead of a Lullaby"
Western Humanities Review	"Cryptozoologist"

"Your Father at Fourteen" won the 2016 Vice Chancellor's International Poetry Prize, and "The Angel in Charge of Creating Earth Addresses His Cohort" won the 2018 Vice Chancellor's International Poetry Prize.

"How to Die, and When" won the 2018 Page Davidson Clayton Prize for Emerging Poets.

"Works and Days" won the 2018 Chad Walsh Poetry Prize, and was republished in *The Orison Anthology*.

"The Burden of Humans" was republished on *Poetry Daily*.

Many thanks to teachers, mentors, readers, and friends: Lance Larsen, Susan Howe, Kimberly Johnson, John Talbot, Mary Jo Salter, Dave Smith, Malachi Black, Claire Wahmanholm, Adam Giannelli, and Sidney Wade. Thanks to everyone at University of Tampa Press, especially Richard Mathews for much hard work making this book better. Deepest gratitude to Jacqueline Osherow for her passion, wisdom, and support. And, of course, everlasting love and gratitude to Claire Akebrand, for everything.

About the Author

Michael Lavers received the Tampa Review Prize for Poetry for *After Earth*, his first booklength collection of poetry. He earned his undergraduate degree from Brigham Young University, an MFA at Johns Hopkins, and a PhD at the University of Utah. His poems have appeared widely in journals including *The Massachusetts Review*, *TriQuarterly*, *AGNI Online*, *Alaska Quarterly Review*, *Georgia Review*, *Antioch Review*, *Hotel Amerika*, *Crazyhorse*, *New Ohio Review*, *Michigan Quarterly Review*, *Beloit Poetry Journal*, *Tampa Review*, *Hayden's Ferry Review*, *Best New Poets 2015*, and *The Hudson Review*. He received the prestigious University of Canberra Vice-Chancellor's International Poetry Prize in 2016 and again in 2018, in addition to earning the *Michigan Quarterly Review* Page Davidson Clayton Prize for Emerging Poets, 2018. Together with his wife, the writer and artist Claire Åkebrand, and their two children, he now lives in Provo, Utah, and teaches poetry at Brigham Young University.

About the Book

After Earth is set in Garamond Premier Pro digital fonts, based on original metal types by Claude Garamond and Robert Granjon that were designed and cast in Paris, France, in the sixteenth century. The contemporary sans serif titling is Agenda, a font designed in the 1990s by independent type designer Greg Thompson, who says it was inspired by Arts and Crafts lettering and "offers warmth in a classic sans serif." The book was designed and typeset by Richard Mathews at the University of Tampa Press.

Made in the USA
Coppell, TX
20 December 2019